T0194768

APOCALYPSE
THEN
AND
NOW

THE BOOK OF
REVELATION REVEALED

ROBERT F. CAMPBELL

WESTBOW
PRESS®
A DIVISION OF THOMAS NELSON
& ZONDERVAN

This book is a work of non-fiction. Unless otherwise noted, the author
and the publisher make no explicit guarantees as to the accuracy of
the information contained in this book and in some cases, names
of people and places have been altered to protect their privacy.

WestBow Press books may be ordered through booksellers or by contacting:

WestBow Press
A Division of Thomas Nelson & Zondervan
1663 Liberty Drive
Bloomington, IN 47403
www.westbowpress.com
844-714-3454

Because of the dynamic nature of the Internet, any web addresses or
links contained in this book may have changed since publication and
may no longer be valid. The views expressed in this work are solely those
of the author and do not necessarily reflect the views of the publisher,
and the publisher hereby disclaims any responsibility for them.

Any people depicted in stock imagery provided by Getty Images are models,
and such images are being used for illustrative purposes only.
Certain stock imagery © Getty Images.

Scripture quotations marked KJV are taken from the King James Version.

ISBN: 979-8-3850-0221-4 (sc)
ISBN: 979-8-3850-0220-7 (e)

Library of Congress Control Number: 2023912684

Print information available on the last page.

WestBow Press rev. date: 01/26/2024

PREFACE

Being raised a Catholic and attending Church and Sunday school for the first twelve years of my life, I was introduced to God at an early age, as I'm sure some of you were. My mother gave my brothers and me a solid foundation to endure life's challenges. I am so grateful for that solid foundation of belief. As time marched on, she herself stopped going to church for her own reasons. However, she still is an inspiration for me wanting to gain an understanding of the teachings of not only Jesus Christ but other religions as they relate to humanity and how we treat one another. I've always been fascinated with the story of God and how humankind came to be. My entire life has been an effort to understand who we are, why we exist, and where and how God fits into all of this.

My brothers and I were altar boys for a time. My parents were not affluent but managed to send us to Catholic school. After the first year, we were given a choice to stay. We opted out and received the rest of our education from the District of Columbia public school system, and we were just fine with that. Somewhere in the eleventh grade, I was given a choice. Not having enough credits to be in the eleventh or tenth grade, I could either go back to junior high school or tread my own path. I decided that school might not be my thing after all and signed up with Job Corps. After three months of training at the Job Corps in West Virginia, I was kicked out for misbehaving, and suddenly found myself at a crossroads for the very first time in my young life.

I thought about it for a while and I decided the military would be my next choice. It should make a man out of me or at the least provide me with a set of skills from which I could make a living and raise a family. In 1978, I got my GED, enlisted, and began my career with the United States Army; that lasted until 2008. The first three years, I was in the regular army, but the last twenty-seven I was in the National Guard and boy what a good decision that was because over the years I was introduced to different cultures and different religions, and I travelled the world on Uncle Sam's dime!

During my time in the military, I was able to follow up on my earlier lessons about Christianity, and one of the books that stood out was Revelation. Truth be told, I was afraid to read it, having heard of its horrors. I still managed to read it several times, even once by candlelight. It was scary and confusing and gave me a sense of the future that predicted doom for humanity. Needless to say, I was hooked and I read it over and over again, each time gleaning something new that I had missed. At the same time, I would refer back to the Bible (King James Version) to validate the end of day's prophecies as described in this book.

Let's flash forward to the year 2020. At the time, I was what I considered a learned gentleman. I had become a warrant officer in the United States Army. I acquired a degree in electrical engineering along with my own Energy Services Company (ESCO), amongst other things. I decided to revisit Revelation, looking at it through the eyes of a sixty year "young" man surviving the loss of a loving wife and having and appreciating the love of his only son. I began to document my thoughts on this most thrilling, albeit disastrous, of possible outcomes for the end of humanity.

I'm writing this book to give me clarity and to finish up on my previous studies. It just so happens that each time I've read this book, I've picked up things I didn't see before. Since from my point of view I'm closer to the end than the beginning, I'd like to get my soul right and prepare as much as I can for whatever awaits me, even if it's only in my mind.

I started writing this book in earnest in early November 2020 and finished in late May 2021. At that time, the world was in the grips of the coronavirus, otherwise known as COVID-19. I did have some time on my hands for contemplation. I must say writing has been quite an eye-opening experience. Now I understand one of the perks of writing. It forces you to look within and either stand by your convictions or have the courage to accept the fact that maybe you didn't know as much as you thought you did after all, then getting through it and moving on to accept new beliefs and concepts. Quite gratifying, I must say.

King James was my primary reference but I did reach out to different versions of the Bible. I looked at the opinions of some scholars and historians available via the internet. Thank God for the internet and, at the same time, be wary of what you read. However, it's good to read other people's thoughts and ideas on a subject. I remember having discussions with people of different religions about their faiths and beliefs and how God fits into their universe. I just remember to keep an open mind whenever I have discussions about God. I believe I have been able to do that during the course of my research for this book. After countless notes and comparing my research with the research of others, I've recorded my thoughts, opinions, and conclusions to this mysterious and yet compelling story of the end of time. I'd like to share these and think you'll find them just as fascinating as I did. Use your own judgment, don't take offense, and after that, just let the words speak to your mind, your soul, and above all your spirit.

Have a good journey!

OPENING

The Book of Revelation opens with John the apostle, writing to the seven churches in Asia Minor. Jesus Christ, through his angel, gives John a vision of the future. Jesus Christ sends a message of repentance to each church. The letters commend the churches for their strengths, but also reminds them of their flaws. These are the same strengths and flaws churches have experienced throughout history. They apply today as they did yesterday. Historians believe John was in exile on the Isle of Patmos in the Aegean Sea off the coast of Turkey, part of a chain of Greek islands. He was sent there by the Romans somewhere between AD 90 and 95 for his witness of the Gospel of Jesus Christ. This meant that John was in the twilight of his life. He was the only original apostle who was not killed for his faith. He was called by Jesus to join him along with his brother James on the shores of Galilee. John was known as the disciple Jesus loved. He was the only disciple who was present when Christ was crucified.

These seven churches—Ephesus, Smyrna,

Pergamos, Thyatira, Sardis, Philadelphia, and Laodicea—were located along an ancient trade route in Persia (modern-day Turkey). Being located along this ancient trade route made it easier to disseminate the Revelation of Jesus Christ throughout the land.

This book is full of symbolism. John describes what he sees through the eyes of a man of his time. He sees things he cannot fully comprehend or has never seen before; therefore, he cannot understand how to describe them in terms we (modern people) can understand. He uses the language of yesterday to put context to the images he sees. There also is the possibility that some images were intentionally blurred or their appearance altered so as not to give future societies the ability to foresee, and therefore prepare for, the Apocalypse. As Jesus said, "Watch therefore: for ye know not what hour your Lord doth come" (Matthew 24:42 KJV).

Shortly after the letters to the churches, John finds himself being taken up to heaven where he sees visions of events to come. He describes a throne room with its contents and talks with what appears to be one of the four beasts, which instruct him to come hither to see the lamb (Jesus Christ) open the first of seven seals. Once opened, each seal tells of specific "dooms" that befall humankind. After the seal openings, there are seven trumpet soundings.

After each trumpet, a new set of trials for repentance is given to humankind, but humans do not repent. After the seals and trumpet soundings, the last seven plaques of humankind are revealed by the opening of vials, or what some describe as emptying the contents of bowls of suffering upon humankind.

Revelation talks of three woes that befall humankind during seven years of tribulation. The first woe is a swarm of locusts released from the bottomless pit. Their sting shall torment people who do not have the mark or seal of God upon their foreheads for five months. Their sting shall be as death, but not. The first woe is revealed after the fifth trumpet.

The second woe begins after the sounding of the sixth trumpet. Four angels are released who were bound at the river Euphrates. These angels and their armies, numbering two hundred million, are released to kill a third of humankind.

The third and final woe is revealed after the seventh trumpet sounds. The third woe marks the finishing of God's judgment on sin, when God establishes his kingdom on earth. Within this third woe are the seven vials or bowls of God's wrath.

THE SEAL
OPENINGS

The first of seven seals are opened. The first four seals release what are called the Four Horsemen of the Apocalypse. There is a white, red, black, and pale horse. Upon each sits a rider, who possesses one of God's judgments for humankind. The rider who sits upon the white horse has a bow; with it, he goes forth conquering, just to conquer. The rider who sits upon the red horse possesses a great sword with which to take peace from the Earth so that humans will kill one another. The rider who sits upon the black horse has the power to let loose famine upon the inhabitants of the earth. The fourth and last rider, who sits upon the pale horse, is named death and hell follows him. These four horsemen are given power over one quarter of the Earth—power to kill with sword, with hunger, with death, and with the beasts of the earth. It is believed God is limiting his judgment at this time, giving people a chance to repent.

The fifth seal is opened and John sees beneath the altar the souls of martyrs who died for preaching

God's word and the testimony they held. They cry out in loud voices, "How long O lord, holy and true dost thou not judge and avenge our blood on them that dwell on the earth?" (Revelation 6:10 KJV). Presumably, these are the souls of the Rapture.

The sixth seal opens and a great earthquake occurs, the sun blackens, and the moon turns blood red. The stars fall from heaven "and heaven departed, as a scroll when it is rolled together; and every mountain and island is moved out of their places." (Revelation 6:14. After these earthly and celestial events, humankind hid themselves in caves and cried to the mountains to hide them from God's wrath.

Then John sees four angels holding back the wind from the four corners of the earth until God's people receive his seal. The number of them sealed was 144,000 from the tribes of Israel. Following this, John sees a great multitude in heaven of all nations and people, clothed in white robes with palms in their hands. This crowd is composed of all those who remained faithful throughout the great tribulation. Because they are faithful, God will give them eternal life. *Are these part of the group of people to be raptured?*

The seventh and final seal is opened. There is a silence in heaven for about half an hour. Then seven angels appear with seven trumpets. Now starts the trumpet trials of repentance.

THE SEVEN
TRUMPET
SOUNDINGS

The first trumpet sounds, hail mixed with fire and blood falls on a third of the trees and grasses, and they are burned up. This most likely precedes a food shortage, the death of animals, and famine. This could be tied to the opening of the third seal and the black rider who brings famine upon the earth.

The second trumpet sounds, "and it is as if a great mountain burning with fire has been cast into the sea and the third part of the sea became blood" (Revelation 8:8 KJV). A third part of the creatures in the sea die, and the third part of the ships are destroyed. This second event seems to follow the first by means of a meteor, an asteroid or some earthy or celestial body falling into the sea. It could possibly be a volcanic eruption, which includes another event as described by the hail and fire of the first trumpet. Whether an eruption, a meteor strike or an asteroid, each of these catastrophes contains hail mixed with fire.

The third trumpet sounds and a great star falls

from the sky. Its name is "Wormwood." A third of the rivers, springs, and fresh water become as wormwood. Many people die of the water because they are bitter. This event, again, seems to be part of the first two trumpet blasts. That a new, or a piece of the same, mountain, meteor or asteroid that fell into the sea also falls on a third of the rivers and lakes of humankind seems highly plausible.

The fourth trumpet sounds and a third of the sun, moon, and stars are darkened for one third of the day. Again, this could be a direct result of the previous trumpets, since those events can result in a dust cloud blocking the sun, the moon, and the stars.

The second, third, and fourth trumpets could all be tied to the opening of the sixth seal. After that seal is opened, a great earthquake happens, the sun and moon blacken, and the stars fall from heaven.

The fifth trumpet sounds, and another star falls from heaven. This star appears to be a "being" of sorts, a fallen angel maybe. To him is given the key to the bottomless pit. Revelation states that once the bottomless pit is opened, an army of locust-like creatures swarm the earth. To them is given the power to sting as scorpions do. They are commanded not to hurt the grass nor any green thing, nor any tree, but only those who do not have the seal of God marked in their foreheads. I don't see this as a bad thing but, it will bring about more rebellion from the unbelievers since the sting does not kill but causes five months of agony and pain. It will be as death but not. These locusts are described as having the shapes of horses, with crowns of gold upon their heads, and the faces of men. Their hair is as that of women and they have the teeth of lions. They have breastplates of iron and their wings sound like many chariots or horses running to battle. They have tails like those of scorpions. Revelation states that they have a king over them, the angel of the bottomless pit, whose name in Hebrew is *Abaddon* and in Greek *Apollyon*. Looking at this trumpet in today's terms, one could possibly interpret the locusts and their leader as an attacking army of some sort, which uses some form of chemical or biological warfare to inflict punishment and pain on those who do not have the seal of God.

At this point, we are told, "One woe is past; and behold, there come two woes more hereafter" (Revelation 9:12 KJV).

The sixth trumpet sounds, and the four angels bound in the river Euphrates are released for an hour, a day, a month, and a year to slay a third of humankind. The angels allow the northern invaders to pass across the river Euphrates. It's the army of the two hundred million; they appear as a heavily armed cavalry of sorts. Their power is in their mouths and their tails. It seems this army, along with the swarm of locusts, annihilates another third of humankind. After these plagues, humankind still does not repent; they continue their murders, sorceries, and fornications and their worship of devils and false idols. Here we also read that "the mystery of God should be finished" (Revelation 10:7 KJV). NOW HOW ABOUT THAT!

Then John sees an angel. The angel has in his hand a small open book. He sets one foot on the sea and the other on the land. The angel roars and the seven thunders respond. *(I can't figure out who those seven thunders are.)* A voice from heaven tells John not to write what the seven thunders utter *(I wonder what that was)*. Then the angel swears by God, "There should be time no longer" (Revelation 10:6 KJV), or what some interpret as "no delay," meaning God's mercy is over and judgment day is at hand. The voice from heaven tells John to take the little book from the angel's hand and eat it, saying that it will be bitter in his belly but sweet as honey in his mouth. It appears eating this book gives John the ability to prophesy in different tongues, knowing and speaking all languages.

John is then given a rod to measure the temple of God, the altar, and those who worship therein. There are those who say the temple is symbolic—not a physical place but a spiritual wall of protection for the believers of God. However, John is told not to measure the outer court, that of the Gentiles, because the outer court would be trampled underfoot for three and a half years by the Gentiles. God will appoint two witnesses to prophesy during the second half of tribulation. These witnesses cannot be harmed and have the power to shut up the heavens, withhold rain, turn water to blood, and send plagues as often as they will. If anyone tries to harm them, fire comes out their mouths and consumes them. When they finish their ministry, the beast (antichrist) kills them. Their bodies will lie in the street for three days. The people shall rejoice over their deaths since they tormented them with their words as well as their supernatural powers. After three days, the two witnesses will ascend to heaven and fear shall fall upon those who dwell on the earth. God raptures his two witnesses. This display of power causes an earthquake that levels one tenth of the city of Jerusalem and snuffs out seven thousand people. After this display of power, panic grips the survivors who ascribe glory to God but do not worship or honor him.

Now we read, "The second woe is past; and behold, the third cometh quickly (Revelation 11:14 KJV).

The seventh trumpet sounds and there are voices in heaven saying, "The kingdoms of this world have become the kingdoms of our lord and of his Christ; and he shall reign forever and ever" (Revelation 11:15 KJV). Then the temple of God in heaven opens. Within it is the ark of his testament. There is lightning, voices, thundering, an earthquake, and great hail. The seventh trumpet ushers in the vial or bowl judgments, as they are sometimes called. However, before we get to them, John tells us of a sign that appears in heaven: a woman clothed with the sun and the moon under her feet. Upon her head is a crown of twelve stars. She, being with child cried, travailing in birth, and pained to be delivered. (Revelation 12:1 KJV)

This part of Revelation is filled with symbolism. The woman represents Israel. A red dragon (the Devil) appears, the woman gives birth to a son (Jesus Christ), and the dragon tries to consume it. However, God snatches the baby up and hides the woman from the dragon for 1260 days (three and a half years). Now, things shift again to a war in heaven between Michael and the dragon. Michael ultimately wins and the devil is cast down to earth along with his angels. Some scholars believe the expulsion of Satan described here refers to his initial rebellion against God before the dawn of humankind. This is another one of those shifting events throughout Revelation that's confusing yet necessary in content and visual imagery.

Now, John sees a beast rising from the sea. It

has seven heads and ten horns. Upon the horns are ten crowns and upon the heads was the name of blasphemy (this could be the worldly powers typified by the beast who denies the divinity of God). There is a belief that the ten crowns represent ten kings or rulers yet to be and the seven heads are the Seven Hills of Rome. Since the beast comes out the sea, some believe it probably will be in the Mediterranean region, let's say somewhere in Europe, that gives birth to the beast. The sea could also represent the restless mass of humankind. John sees that one of the beast's heads is wounded as to death. His deadly wound is healed, and all the world wonders about the beast and worships the dragon that gave power to the beast. Power is given to the beast to continue forty and two months (three and a half years). That means the beast is revealed somewhere in the middle of the tribulation. This first beast is the antichrist.

Another beast comes out of the earth at this time. He has two horns and speaks as the dragon did. Some believe he will arise from Israel since he comes from the land. He is the false prophet who will cause everyone to worship the image (statue) of the first beast that he caused to speak. This statue may be located presumably in the holy of holies. Now we know this is possible because of robotics, so it is quite believable that John saw and heard the statue of the beast speak.

Together these three—the dragon, the antichrist, and the false prophet form an unholy trinity in direct opposition to God the father, the son, and the Holy Spirit.

The second beast causes humanity to receive the mark of the beast on either their right hand or forehead. Without it, a person cannot buy or sell anything. *(Beware of a time when humans are forced to allow the insertion of some kind of digital processing device into the body.)* The final verse in chapter 13 introduces us to the person who supposedly is responsible for raining down hell upon the earth. John records, "Let him that hath understanding count the number of the beast: for it is the number of a man; and his number is Six hundred threescore and six" (Revelation 13:18 KJV). This is the beast and his number is 666.

Then John looks and beholds a lamb on Mount Zion. With him are 144,000 of the faithful, having his father's name written on their foreheads. This 144,000 are the same group of 144,000 Jews saved in chapter 7. They received the seal of God on their foreheads. They ministered faithfully during the first part of Revelation and probably fled to a place of safety for the second half. Of the twelve tribes of Israel that received the seal of God, the tribe of Dan is not mentioned. It seems the tribe of Dan may have worshiped idols alongside the tribe of Ephraim. Next John sees three angels in heaven. The first announces God's willingness to accept anyone who will believe in him. This is the last chance at repentance before God's wrath befalls humankind. A second angel follows and says, "Fallen! fallen is Babylon the Great" (Revelation 14:8 NIV). The third angel lets the unbelievers who have the mark of the beast know they shall suffer the same death as the beast.

Then John looks and beholds "a white cloud, and upon the cloud one sat like unto the son of man, having on his head a golden crown, and in his hand a sharp sickle" (Revelation 14:14 KJV). John then sees another angel come out of the temple, crying with a loud voice to the man who sits on the cloud, "Thrust in thy sickle and reap for the time is come for thee to reap; for the harvest of the earth is ripe" (Revelation 14:15 KJV). Another angel comes out of the temple with a sickle used to harvest the unbelievers. Another comes from the altar. He has the charge of fire, and tells the angel with the sickle, "Thrust in thy sharp sickle, and gather the clusters of the vine of the earth, for her grapes are fully ripe" (Revelation 14:18 KJV).

The third woe has arrived.

John sees seven angels appear in heaven with the last plagues of humankind. There is no repentance once the angels start to unleash or pour God's wrath upon the remnants of humankind.

The first angel opens his vial and there fell a noisome and grievous sore upon the people who had the mark of beast and worshipped his image. *Could these sores come from the sting of the locust?*

The second angel empties his vial in the sea and it becomes blood; everything living in the sea dies. *Could this be a continuation or part of the opening of the second seal when a great mountain was cast into the sea and the sea became as blood?*

"The third angel pours his vial upon the rivers and fountains of water, and they also become blood." (Revelation 16:4 KJV). *Could this tie into the fourth seal when the star WORMWOOD fell on the rivers and fountains and made them bitter?*

The fourth angel opens his vial and pours it upon the sun. Power is given to him to scorch humans with fire and great heat. *Could this be a nuclear explosion or many explosions?* Still, humans do not repent.

The fifth angel pours the contents of his vial upon the seat of power of the beast. Darkness falls upon his kingdom and the people gnaw their tongues but do not repent. *Could this be part of the aftermath of a nuclear explosion when large amounts of dust are kicked up into the atmosphere, preventing sunlight from reaching the earth's surface?*

The sixth angel pours his vial upon the Euphrates River to dry it up and make ready the path for the kings of the east. *Could this be part of the sixth trumpet, when the army of the 200 million crosses the Euphrates River?*

Then John sees three unclean spirits that appear to be frogs coming out of the mouths of the dragon, the beast, and the false prophet. Their job is to gather the kings of the earth to a place called Armageddon. This battlefield is located near the city of Meggiddo, which is a large plain in northern Israel (southeast of the modern port of Haifa). Meggiddo was one of the three cities that guarded the Via Maris trade route. Standing near a critical mountain pass, it was the most strategic location of a well-traveled road in ancient times.

There is no reason at this time, why these armies will gather. It most likely is not to fight the beast, who is presumably an ally. Then what is the purpose? Some believe it may be an all-out attempt to destroy the Jews or maybe these armies will come because of some sort of resource that's discovered in the region.

The seventh and final angel pours his vial into the air. A great voice speaks from the throne inside the temple of heaven, saying, "It is done" (Revelation 16:17 KJV). After the final vial is poured on humankind, an earthquake as never seen or heard of before shakes the earth and mountains fall, seas disappear, and the entire earth's continents are reconfigured. The great city (presumably Jerusalem) splits into three, and Babylon also falls. Every island disappears and the mountains are leveled. This final plague also brings hailstones about the size of talents, which each weighed seventy-five pounds. These stones pummeled the people of the earth.

One of the seven angels who had the seven vials comes to John and says, "Come hither, I will shew unto thee the judgment of the great whore that sits on many waters" (Revelation 17:1 KJV). John is taken away in the spirit to the wilderness where he sees a woman (presumably Israel) sitting on a scarlet beast full of names of blasphemy, seven heads, and ten horns. The woman has had written on her forehead, MYSTERY BABYLON THE GREAT, THE MOTHER OF HARLOTS AND ABOMINATIONS OF THE EARTH (Revelation 17:5 KJV). The angel tells John the mystery of the beast upon which the woman sits. The beast proceeded out of the bottomless pit. The seven heads are seven mountains upon which the woman sits (Rome or the Catholic Church). There are seven kings, five of which have fallen, one is, and the other is yet to come. The beast that was and is not, is the eighth and of the seventh and shall go into perdition.

The ten horns are ten kings who will receive power but for an hour with the beast. They are of one mind and will give their power to the beast. They will be defeated by the lamb. "And the ten horns which thou sawest upon the beast, these shall hate the whore and shall make her desolate and naked and shall eat her flesh, and burn her with fire. "(Revelation 17:16 KJV).

This entire seventeenth chapter seems to allude to a world system of government/religion that is ungodly and is referred to as Babylon. However, the beast and his cohorts are threatened by its popularity and destroy it. This is what evil does: it consumes itself. This happens in the middle of tribulation when the beast comes to power, assumes the role of God, and demands that everyone worship him.

After this, John sees another angel descending from heaven who has great authority and illuminates the entire earth. He pronounces that Babylon the great has fallen. Then John hears another voice from heaven saying, "Come out of her my people, that ye not be partakers of her sins and that ye receive not of her plagues" (Revelation 18:4 KJV).

Chapter 18 describes in detail the fall of Babylon. This Babylon, unlike the previous religious Babylon, is the seat of political, commercial, and economic power. It will be destroyed in one hour by famine, death, mourning, and fire. The kings of the earth will mourn Babylon from a distance so as not to be consumed themselves. No one knows exactly where this city is. Some say it will be somewhere near the Euphrates River and some say it is a symbolic place.

After the destruction of Babylon, John hears a multitude of voices in heaven rejoicing about the marriage of the bride (church) and the bridegroom (Jesus Christ). Then John sees heaven open up and a rider on a white horse (Jesus Christ). This is the second coming of Jesus Christ. Jesus returns as a conqueror, not as a lamb as before. Following him are his armies and on his head is a name that no one knows but himself. Out of his mouth comes a sharp two-edged sword that he uses to smite the nations of people. Since this sword of the lord is his words, it is reasonable to assume Jesus will smite his foes with but a word. This seems to follow a verse in St John, which states, "In the beginning was the word and the word was with God, and the word was God" (St John 1:1-2 KJV).

Then John sees an angel standing in the sun, who cries out in a loud voice to all the fowls that fly in the midst of heaven, "Come and gather yourselves together unto the supper of the great God; That ye may eat the flesh of kings, and the flesh of captains, and the flesh of mighty men" (Revelation 19:17–18

KJV). Then John sees the beast and the kings of the earth and their armies gathered together in a futile attempt to make war with Jesus Christ. This is the final battle, the battle of Armageddon. John sees the beast and the false prophet captured and thrown into the lake of fire. Then Jesus smites their armies with the spoken word. Afterward, the fowl of the air feast upon their corpses.

John then sees an angel descending from heaven with the key to the bottomless pit and a great chain in his hand. With it, he binds the dragon (the devil) for a thousand years and sets a seal on him, so he will not deceive the nations anymore until the thousand years have passed. Then the dragon will be released again, but only for a short while. There are those who don't understand why God does this. It may be to prove that even after a thousand years of peace and harmony, some humans will still have the capacity for evil and reject the word of God. However, those who do, will die the second death and be thrown into the lake of fire.

John sees thrones; those sitting on them have the power for judgment. He sees the souls of those who were beheaded for witnessing about Jesus Christ. They will live and reign with Jesus Christ for a thousand years. The rest of the dead do not live again until the thousand years have passed. This is the first resurrection upon which the second death has no power. After the thousand years, Satan will gather his armies from the four corners of the earth from the lands of Gog and Magog. These lands could very well be Persia, Ethiopia, and Libya. Then there is Gomer and all his bands from the northern quarters, parts of Europe and Turkey. However, God causes hail fire to rain down and consume their armies. The devil is cast into the lake of fire where the beast and false prophet are to be tormented forever.

THE FINAL
JUDGMENT

John sees a great white throne and the one who sits on it. He sees the dead; "small and great stand before God and the books were opened, and another book was opened, the book of life: and the dead were judged out of those things which were written in the books, according to their works" (Revelation 20:12 KJV). The sea gives up its dead and death and hell deliver up their dead. Everyone is judged according to his or her works. Then death and hell are cast into the lake of fire. This is the second death. Whoever's name was not written in the book of life was cast into the lake of fire.

John then sees a new heaven and a new earth because the first two have passed away. John states he sees the holy city, the New Jerusalem, coming down from God out of heaven. John hears a voice saying, "Behold the tabernacle of God is with men, and he will dwell with them" (Revelation 21:3 KJV). There will be no more death or sorrow. Then he who sits on the throne says, "It is done, I am the Alpha and the Omega, the beginning and the End. I will give unto him that is athirst of the fountain of the water of life freely" (Revelation 21:6 KJV). The last part of chapter 21 talks symbolically about how the holy city looks. Then one of the angels that poured the bowls of judgment takes John away into the spirit and shows him the New Jerusalem.

The last chapter of Revelation describes what is inside the new holy city. For the first time, we will see our maker, God. However, the text also warns anyone who would add or take away from the Book of Revelation and reminds them they will spend eternity in the lake of fire. In Closing:

"Blessed are they that do his commandments that they may have right to the tree of life and may enter in through the gates into the city." (Revelation 22:14 KJV)

Jesus says, "I am the root and the offspring of David, and the bright and morning star." (Revelation 22:16 KJV)

"And the spirit and the bride say, come. And let him that heareth say, come. And let him that is athirst, come. And whosoever will, let him take of the water of life freely." (Revelation 22:17 KJV)

May the grace of our Lord Jesus Christ be with you all. Amen.

CONCLUSION

Having completed my research and finishing this book, I've come to the conclusion that I hope I'm not around for the end of days, if such a time actually unfolds as described in the Book of Revelation. Life is hard enough as it is, without the three woes befalling us and destroying not only humankind but the entire earth as well.

We will be judged at the end by how we conduct ourselves during this most terrible time and will be held accountable for our actions throughout our entire lives as well.

Something as devastating as described in Revelation is almost incomprehensible. I guess that's why most people, including me, hesitated to read it or found it so disturbing because of its prophecy of ultimate doom.

After writing this book, it is my belief that sometime in the not-too-distant future humankind, along with Mother Nature and, of course, by the will of God, will conspire to bring about such events as described in this book. It is quite comprehensible to believe some of the events described in the Book of Revelation. Take, for instance, "the mark of the beast." This could be at work right now. We seem to be moving toward a system of buying and selling that revolves around expedience and convenience. It uses technology that can be inserted into our bodies. The mark of the beast could be closer than we think.

One simple, or not too simple, catastrophe could start the turmoil of tribulation in motion. Imagine a massive earthquake or two, throw in a volcano explosion or two, maybe a tsunami on top of that, and we are in it. Our societies are ill equipped to manage events of such magnitude. Massive famine and suffering would surely follow, with only the people with the seal of God protected, according to Revelation. Most other people who survive will be forced to make a choice between living and dying, eating and starving, based on their affiliations or lack thereof. Hence, the mark of the beast may be the only means of survival for most people during this period.

This is not to mention the other horrors of tribulation: the wars, the plagues, the hatred human beings will exhibit toward each other and their inability to save themselves from the wrath of God. These happenings can push most people over the edge into a world devoid of any empathy and compassion for our fellow human beings. Such a time, I surely hope, I'm not around to see.

Though some of the events described in the Book of Revelation seem spiritual rather than physical, and I'm sure in some cases they are, you can't help but see how some of the events could actually befall us, minus the spiritual connection. As I said, a few natural catastrophes and we are in it, knee deep. Most of the events that befall the inhabitants of Earth during this time seem to stem from a catastrophic event or two that makes living conditions almost intolerable, especially because food and water will be in short supply. Whoever has those things, and the means to keep them, will control everyone else. The actions of what's left of our society following these events probably will end up bringing about the rest of the calamity of Revelation. It's kind of in our nature to behave just as Revelation describes during a time of such great sorrow or Tribulation.

I'd like to believe the agony and pain of tribulation will bring about an "awakening of humanity" that can only be achieved by (sorry to say) great suffering. It is said that a person rises from the bottom of his or her sorrows to his or her higher self. If that's the case, tribulation is the vehicle that should get us there, whether we want to go or not.

As a note, I've always found Genesis 3:17–19 quite interesting. This passage describes the path that each human must endure while they sojourner through life.

Adam's sin brought the curse of laborious work and death on the human race. When Adam sinned, God told him,

> "Because thou hast hearkened unto the voice of thy wife, and hast eaten of the tree, of which I commanded thee, saying, thou shalt not eat of it: Cursed is the ground for thy sake; in sorrow shalt thou eat of it all the days of thy life; thorns also and thistles it shall bring forth to thee; and thou shalt eat the herbs of the field; in the sweat of thy face shalt thou eat bread, till thou return unto the ground, for out of it wast thou taken; for dust thou art and unto dust shalt thou return." (Genesis 3:17–19)

Printed in the United States
by Baker & Taylor Publisher Services